COMMAND YOUR PRESENCE

A guide to effective sales communication online and offline

Kenyetta L Gordon

© *Copyright 2020*

All rights reserved

All rights to this book are reserved. No permission is given for any part of this book to be reproduced, transmitted in any form or means; electronic or mechanical, stored in a retrieval system, photocopied, recorded, scanned, or otherwise. Any of these actions require the proper written permission of the publisher.

Disclaimer 6

INTRODUCTION 7

CHAPTER ONE 9

IS YOUR BRAND AN AUTHORITY? 9

CHAPTER TWO 17

PERSONAL DEVELOPMENT- CAMERA AND PUBLIC SPEAKING CONFIDENCE 17

   How can I get better as a public speaker? 19

CHAPTER THREE 27

WORD STRESS IN YOUR SPEECH 27

   Intonation and its Effects on your Audience 32

CHAPTER FOUR 36

UNDERSTANDING YOUR AUDIENCE- THE PSYCHOLOGY OF COMMUNICATION 36

Psychological Schools of Thought on Communication 38

   Understanding your Audience 40

CONCLUSION 48

Disclaimer

All knowledge contained in this book is given for informational and educational purposes only. The author is not in any way accountable for any results or outcomes that emanate from using this material. Constructive attempts have been made to provide information that is both accurate and effective, but the author is not bound for the accuracy or use/misuse of this information.

INTRODUCTION

Communication, over the years, has been a force to reckon with at every level of life and human existence; humans as well as other animate objects need to communicate to survive and regenerate. Life altogether would be quiet, boring, and at a stand-still if all we as humans did was wake up, move like mutes not observing and recognizing the existence of others and then returned to bed in a similar cycle till the world ends.

Language- both verbal (comprising sounds, letters and words) and nonverbal (comprising gestures and body movements) were established from the beginning of human creation for the purpose of living a meaningful, organized life, and especially, to have a better interpersonal relationship.

In recent times, communication has been featured in so many success stories of individuals, brand owners and corporate organizations who depend on external audiences to establish their ventures. However, an effective communication strategy and procedure has generated more results in this aspect.

The purpose of this guide is to provide the most summarized detailed tips and recommendations to achieving success in dealing with your audience while consulting them to make a financial decision in the interest of your brand. Apart from this, it will open your eyes to the understanding of your customers/audience, but importantly, building your brand to levels of becoming an authority in your niche.

CHAPTER ONE

IS YOUR BRAND AN AUTHORITY?

"Your premium brand had better be delivering something special, or it is not going to get the business" - **Warren Buffett**

Addressing an audience is usually the hammer used to hit the nail on the head- the head of the nail, however, is the specific purpose of the address. Public speaking is usually for an important purpose, either to inform, educate, direct, or consult the audience or listeners to make a particular decision. In this context, you are a brand owner, a marketer, a public speaker, or a sales consultant aiming for the positive response of the audience- your potential customers- and the decision they would make in the favor of your proposition.

How established are you as a representative of a brand?

The question is - is your brand an authority that people would spend their time, money, and attention to listen to? Is your brand worth their time and energy, and consequently the decision you are looking forward to them taking? How actively have you attempted to improve your brand to make its tone a valuable one?

The major goal you want to hit with your brand is to make it likeable, personable, and relatable. Below are a few tips to make your brand earn itself a place in the hearts of your potential customers:

Your keyword is top-notch: Marketing nowadays is fast running and many are finding it hard to catch up with its pace. Nevertheless, there is still a huge crowd out there trying to sell the same thing that you are selling; one of the ways to have an edge over the competition is to aim at delivering beyond expectations. A major factor that beats competition and proclaims a brand is what their customers get in return for their money. The quality of their delivery, the form of experience they had during the transaction, and how professional the brand portrays itself during the transaction.

Reveal personalities: Humans tend to hand over their trust when there is something to hold on to for the assurance of their financial commitment. Research has it that brands which have at one point or the other revealed the personalities behind the name, logo, and taglines have experienced more trust than brands in which their potential customers have no extra knowledge of them. Doing this in intervals through any relevant means, create an opportunity for engagement and relationships between the brand and your customers by assuring them that they are dealing with humans like them who understand their plights, concerns, and expectations.

Think outside the box: It is usually not enough for a brand to attempt to relate with their customers alone by revealing the brain behind the product they love or the services they have been enjoying. It is strongly advised that you tailor your content, identity, and activities to link up with the emotional part of your audience; understand and relate your message with the various emotions of your audience. Inform them that you are aware that there is an emotional part of them, and your brand is set to appease such emotion.

Your strengths first: Another aspect you want your customers to know more of is how established you are as a brand, your level of experience, how much you offer in your service, and how much more you are ready to deliver more than you have previously delivered. You want to share your success stories first before any other thing. Assure them first before they come across any element of doubt.

Be valuable: Customers often go out of their way to compare brands before making certain decisions. This calls for the need to assure them of how valuable your brand can be to them. This can be done by delivering way above what your competitors are delivering. In the case of unavoidably retaining the same price, you can always increase the value your deliveries give your customers each time they pay for your goods or services. Be sure to give more than what they can get from others.

Be unique: while I cannot overemphasize the need to always do market research, study your competitors, etc., there is also a more critical need to create your own statement and stick to it. As I always say, *"Branding is telling your story to the audience before the audience tells it for you. Therefore, it begins at inception."* Nothing beats being original, let your craft be assigned to you and you alone. Deviating from this will mix your brand up in the market and you will eventually get lost in the crowd with no unique mark to identify or differentiate you from the others; originality is the key.

Have you tried consistency? Do you realize people, majority of times, are drawn to brands that have registered a particular percentage of information in their minds already? There will always be a brand that comes to their mind when thinking about a specific product. Why is this the case? Such brands have at one point presented themselves to these people more than once with different messages but all pointing at a specific direction. Consistency works like wildfire in the minds of people when something specific comes out of your brand that particularly reminds them of something unforgettable- your core value, no deviation, identification would be easily achievable in the midst of options if they already have a part of your brand in their subconscious. The key is to be consistent while avoiding repetition.

Share the good news where it can be seen: At this stage, every other thing now matters less if this is not taken seriously. It does not matter how standard and enriched your pitch is, if it is not placed where your potential customers are, it is as good as not working on anything for the audience. The most important part of preparing to draw potential customers to your brand is the aspect of your brand visibility. How many times would your brand be suggested when a targeted search is being carried out by an interested customer? You want to get the word out massively into every corner to make people see the goodness you are cooking with your brand. Without this, whatever value you are planning to deliver to your customers would remain with you alone.

Apart from these tips I have shared, there are so many other effective ways you can position your brand or business in a way that the respect your brand deserves will never be taken somewhere else. While preparing to be influential, recognized, and a trusted public speaker, prepare your brand in the best way possible and you will be confident to consult your audience in what you do proudly with enough confidence.

CHAPTER TWO

PERSONAL DEVELOPMENT- CAMERA AND PUBLIC SPEAKING CONFIDENCE

"Effective communication is 20% what you know and 80% how you feel about what you know"

-Jim Rohn

Effective communication (which is way bigger and different from the everyday communication that yields little result) is a combination of two elements- the first being just 20% of what you have studied, your level of experience, what you've planned to deliver, and the other 80% is a sum of how you intend on presenting this knowledge of yours, how many words you intend on using to describe this experience, and how well you are aiming to describe this knowledge in the best way.

Effective communication could be seen as the only vaccine available to cure your dying audience of the disease called misinformation. Would you risk losing this vaccine on your way to the hospital? Would you risk keeping some of the contents behind and taking the half-filled tube to the patient?

Contemporarily, industries and brands now hold social proofs in high esteem as an ace for massively convincing doubting audience. Because of the digitization of things, consumers now prefer to go online to have a human describe what they are looking to venture into or sit under the same roof with brand owners personally describing their products, services, or ventures. By the way, social proofs are pieces of evidence that you have to provide to show that people have used your services and enjoyed it.

Do you shiver when it is time to personally describe to your audience what would help them make significant financial commitments to your business and boost your ROI unimaginably? How hard have you tried to improve yourself when it comes to facing more than ten prospects but to no avail? Here are some proven tips to help you grow beyond the fear and inadequacies of finding it hard to take your position and address the crowd:

How can I get better as a public speaker?

There is absolutely no problem with being nervous: Being nervous is allowed. It is an unavoidable feature in some humans; allow your anxiety to have its cue first and then push it aside with one of the many positive assurances we will discuss later. Curb the anxiety before you make your first sentence, but never try to ignore the fact that you can be anxious of who your unseen audience are (over a camera session). It sometimes gets worse when it is a physical meeting with anticipating and eager audience in a hall and knowing everyone is looking up to you to say the first word.

Learn to be a careful slow talker: It is the best practice to learn and attempt to speak slowly first then beginning on a fast note. Of course, it is understandable that your pace might change automatically as you go deeper in the spirit of talking, but while still at the conscious and controllable level, attempt to select your words carefully and at your most comfortable pace. Fast talkers are not always the best talkers; the best talkers are those who have perfectly passed their messages across, and genuine comprehension followed. It is never a matter of how fast, but how well you deliver the content.

Do the mirror practice: Set aside a large wall mirror in the corner of your room and get to work! Before you step out to address your audience or go into a room lit with studio lights and cameras pointing at you like dreadful guns, dress up in the exact way you would dress when you are on the stage, take your position and speak confidently at the mirror as though it is a camera recording your every move. This practice has proven to build confidence over the years. It is a strategic practice that most people use, which has resulted in them blowing their audience's minds! This practice would lead us to the next tip.

Rehearse and record yourself before the actual presentation date: While using the mirror method or any other means, always take a good time to rehearse whatever points you have gathered. Utilize an audio or video recorder and see how well you performed during the rehearsal. Do this often until you are confident enough that you are ready to step out and hit it.

Avoid memorizing: As disagreeable as this may sound, it is in your best interest to only understand your point than to learn that paragraph in your notepad. There is always a large extent to which you can discuss what you already understand than what you have memorized. This practice is a piece of advice because distractions are bound to occur during your presentation, and unconsciously, your memorized lines will create a distraction. What will you say to your audience at that time? "Err… excuse me", "…ok, let's skip that!"?

You are the boss: Knowing this key is the essential factor that keeps public speakers going on a high. There would be no false assumption anywhere if you see yourself as the authority; the whole audience has gathered to listen to you. Of course, they trust you with whatever is about to come out of your mouth.

You have the entire time to yourself to feed your audience with your content without objection. They believe you know more on the topic of matter than they do, hence their rapt attention before you start talking. Do you see yourself this way? This confidence booster is a significant boost to the spirit and generates extreme confidence on the stage.

The thirty second rule: Make it a habit to take a series of deep breaths every thirty seconds before going live on the camera. Doing this helps reduce the unavoidable tension that comes with facing the crowd. The best part about recording is, you can always edit the final product to be published. In the case of a physical public speaking where your audience is seated and ready to hear from you, take your first thirty seconds to stand still, smile, take deep breaths, and say the positive words of assurance to yourself. For example: *"I can do this. I know my craft and I am a master at this. They have come to hear from me. I will* *not fail, and I will not disappoint myself or my audience. So, let's do this!"* Say these in your mind and then shoot!

The camera gives relaxation and comfort: Have you thought otherwise before now? The camera is just a transmitter of your emotions, feelings, and behavior to the audience. It is the first reminder that you are meant to be in your best state. So be as comfortable as possible. You must know that the emotions attached to your words will affect the mood of your audience? Give your audience your best self while giving out the best content you know you can deliver.

Prioritize your audience: During your delivery, try not to get technical or use industry jargon. Remember, you are the expert on this topic, and your audience may not be as knowledgeable on the subject as you. Hence, going too technical and using complicated terms and acronyms would yield your listeners from fully comprehending the knowledge you are trying to deliver. Build personalization and relatability with your audience amid the presentation, use personal pronouns that carry them along, use social proofs to back up your point. Doing this builds trust within your audience and makes you an industry influencer within their eyes.

Smile as you speak: This subconsciously creates a mood within your listeners and gives them a sense of familiarity. So, become conscious of your facial reactions and nonverbal gestures. When you smile while speaking, word stressors and inflections begin to arise that would assist in passing your message across automatically. Recognizing what words to inflect when speaking allows your listener to savor the topic at hand and the points they must reflect on. Think of it like eating a steak with fat versus eating a steak without fat. One truly allows you to savor the flavors, while the other does not entirely give you the full enjoyment of recognizing what the chef wanted you to taste. Understanding this tactic results is a soothing of dialogue and understanding on the receiver's end.

These and other important tips that haven't been listed above on the best communicative practice would be discussed at a point subsequently in the guide. Stay tuned!

CHAPTER THREE

WORD STRESS IN YOUR SPEECH

"In writing a weird story, I always try very carefully to achieve the right mood and atmosphere and place the emphasis where it belongs"

-H. P. Lovecraft

Word stress is an essential part of any effective communication. It coverts in the stream of expressions but holds an undeniable role in the success story of any speech. When correctly used when speaking, word stressing helps your listeners to identify words, notice the importance of the topic and tells the listener to hold on to it in mind for a longer time than any other word(s) in the expression. It also helps to distinguish prominence and dictates meanings on the receiving part of the audience.

According to phonetics, word stressors is the amount of emphasis you ascribe to a particular syllable, word, or group of words in the expression. Stress in your speech could be calculated based on how emphatic you were while producing or pronouncing certain parts of the phrase. Now, when addressing your audience (who are also your potential customers), there is a level of emphasis some words which naturally should receive and other words you would emphasize no stress to achieve your aim. Your predominant objective is to make your listener focus on a particular word(s) for a more extended period. Allow their minds to act towards the dictation of the emphasis. Implementing the practice of inflection and word stressing in order to win the hearts or trusts of your audience is the act of delivering subliminal messages to the subconscious part of the mind. This tactic ignites internal reactions of the emphasized word(s) and could allow them to make individual decisions in your favor! Isn't this good?

Now that you have an idea of what word stressing and inflection is and how it can help you achieve your goals, let's take note of how to use it when speaking.

How do we stress words while presenting?

Pronouncing with clarity: Allow yourself to take a few seconds and pronounce particular words you are trying to emphasize. When speaking with clarity, it requires a longer time in seconds for those words more than their actual pronunciation durations and more than the duration allocated to other words in the expression. All that this requires is for us to give special prominence to syllables in words to be stressed to achieve maximum effect. Consider the pronunciation of the capitalized word in the expression:

"Mr. John thought I sold digital products, but I immediately told him I **SHHIIP*** *physical products to any location."*

In the example above, the word *ship* was emphasized to differentiate my service from that of a digital marketer, allowing him to clearly understand that my services are only available when you need a physical shipment.

Pronouncing words with clarity can be achieved in two ways:

- Switching to a rising tone while pronouncing the word

- Spending time on the pronunciation of such words

Giving a distinctive facial expression during the pronunciation of certain words: In a bid to making the audience know that there is a term in your expression that you would like for them to give special preference to you can switch to the use of words with sharp noticeable inflections. Do this while matching facial expression or gesture while pronouncing that word. Doing this can suddenly make an audience curious as to why your countenance has changed, which would meet their curiosity with the source of the sudden change, the emphasized word. See the instance of the conversation used above where the word ship is emphasized, without further explanation, the listener in the conversation would be aware that there is something important in your response when you nod your head affirmatively to pronounce ship.

Then this informs them that you ONLY ship physical products as opposed to digital ones.

Attributing a longer vowel to a word or words:
Similar to pronouncing words with clarity, apart from slowing down while producing the whole word, only the vowels in such word can be stretched to achieve stress or emphasis on them. It also requires spending a longer time in the production, but only differs because the time would be spent on the vowels in the word instead.

Intonation and its Effects on your Audience

Intonation in speech is the conscious or unconscious fluctuation in the rising and falling of your tone. Intonation can be unconsciously introduced in speech when the flow of the communication is on a normal level, and there is almost no reason to tweak your intonation for special effect, while the conscious use of intonation (our concern) is when there is an intentional variation in the rising and falling of the tone while speaking to achieve particular effects.

Do you know that when you use word stress and vary your tone in the appropriate high and low forms, you will achieve three extra things in your audience in the midst of talking?

- Engagement
- Excitement
- Interest

Nothing beats these three things when it comes to motivations during a presentation, once they give you these, you naturally see yourself gliding on a smooth cruise!

Apart from these, intonation helps the process of meaning suggesting, meaning interpretation, and meaning-making on the part of your audience. Also, the audience tends to see you as being confident and being the authority they have come to listen to when you end your sentences on a falling tone. It naturally depicts assurance, conviction, confidence, and truth.

On the other hand, if most or all of your sentences end with rising or high tones, the audience would perceive you to be unsure, anxious, lacking confidence, and unable to back whatever is coming out of your mouth up. Consider the sentences below and imagine what you, as a reader could perceive after the utterances.

1. What WOULD YOU like us to do?
2. What would you LIKE US to do?
3. What would you like us to do?

What do you perceive from these three expressions? Observe the ones capitalized to indicate stress and a rising tone, and also compare the last without a rising tone. We could perceive the following:

1. An offensive statement
2. A caring statement
3. An apathetic statement

Are the effects of our intonation and how audience are likely to interpret them understood now?

CHAPTER FOUR

UNDERSTANDING YOUR AUDIENCE- THE PSYCHOLOGY OF COMMUNICATION

"A person standing in front of an audience without enthusiasm for his subject and his actions is disconnected from his spirit"

-Wayne Dyer

Marketing is basically an activity that involves a brand owner who tries to meet the demands of people by offering the link between their demands and their satisfaction- his/her product. Marketing is usually audience-centered, in the sense that everything a marketer does is usually tailored to match the desire of the least interested potential customer. But what to do when you have little or no understanding of who you are trying to sell to? It is as good as not having anything to sell. Of what gain is uploading a nice summer picture on an Instagram account with zero followers?

If you don't know who your target audience is, how can you know what marketing strategy to execute? How can you know what message to compose? And how can you tell if the message is the best to send out when there's no target audience in mind? Your audience is the main reason you have a brand; as you build your brand, know who you want to sell to!

Your audience are humans too, therefore, the need to consider their psychological build-ups while planning your speech is expedient. Different people understand the same points differently as a result of their psychological states, experiences, prior beliefs, etc. Generalizing contents for the masses is never a good option in addressing your audience. There are certain psychological schools of thought that have described the different possible situations in their unique ways. Let's consider some of them

Psychological Schools of Thought on Communication

Constructivism: This school of thought believes in the possibility of a group of people to have different capacities to interpret the same message in their various ways. It believes in the need for a speaker to understand his or her audience first and then tailor the content to match the capacities of the various audience.

Cognitive-Behavioral school of thought: This theory believes in the ability of communication to further affect the behavior or way of life of the audience. That being said, the way the audience perceives a message has the ability to affect their behaviors subsequently. In short, communication can effect a change or restructuring in their behaviors. This is implied by the stimulus-response principle where the content of an effective communication is the stimulus that elicits a particular response in the behavioral part of the audience.

Social Judgement Theory: This theory posits that during communication, the audience can either choose to accept a proposition, reject it, or be indifferent about it. And these three possibilities are determined by how important the topic of talk is to them at the moment, that is, their ego involvement at the moment of the communication.

The Spiral of Silence: This is the theory that focuses on the experience of the people who fear isolation, and as a result of the fear of isolation, they tend to retain their minority opinions and stick to the widely opined majority beliefs. According to this school of thought, the fear of isolation causes silence by the minority and sees them accept the majority view at the expense of their personal beliefs.

These schools of thought and many others have postulated various theories in an attempt to reveal the various psychological build-ups of the different types of audience one might come across. Since we are now aware of who our audiences can be, how can we understand who they are precisely for our business strategy?

Understanding your Audience

Here are a few steps you need to take in having a perfect idea of who you are marketing to and how best to push your brand at them:

Accurate Research: An important way to know and understand who your audience is in any business communication is to develop an intense research study before having your presentation. This is quite important when you are addressing a group of people in a common class, this way your research would be a narrowed one and focus would only be on knowing each participant personally. Knowing what triggers their happy button, what pisses them off, their point of views about businesses like yours, etc. In essence, researching your audience's likes and dislikes, areas of interest, etc. would give your strategy enough advantage.

Specific needs of your audience: This works more effectively during the research stage, you want to carry out a Needs Analysis on them to know what it is they actually need and what they require to hear at that point in time. Otherwise, going the other way without understanding the needs of your audience may be toxic to your aim at the end of the communication.

Confirm from your competitors: While trying to make your research, you can stretch your research beyond the large market and go into the base of your competitors, have a glimpse of what they are doing, who they are targeting (since you have the same target audience), how they are targeting these prospects, what they are feeding their potential customers with, and what strategy they are using in marketing their products to their target audience. Please note that while doing this, you might come across a competitor who is actually going the right way, but what you do is only pick what's helpful and leave the rest.

Create your persona: A customer persona is a fictitious character who you give all the assumed personalities of your potential customers. While gathering your demographic data about your audience generally, there will come a time where you have to make an imaginary character with generalized characteristics for the purpose of commercial decision making. After doing the creation of the persona, you want to start relating to the persona exactly as you would do to your actual customers. Please note that this is in a bid to running tests and to compare results with what would work in the real life.

Go personal with your audience: You might need to take a step forward by deviating from the general audience study you have been doing, it is high time you knew your audience individually if it is something you can do easily. This way, you get to understand their personal demographics and can make personal decisions towards satisfying your customers individually. Most importantly, it is after a successful data collation process on individuals that you can make accurate general assumptions.

Monitor audience's responses: If you already have had a brand for some time now, it is of great importance that you pay attention to how your audience engage with your contents, offers, brand decisions, etc. With this, you can know the state of their minds towards your service, you can repeat the best practices and see if good feedback would be retained, this way you can determine what would work and what would not work.

Importance of your tone and mood during presentation

As we have discussed earlier, your audience are humans and have feelings and emotions. Not only can they decide to give their attentions unconsciously when your points are striking a chord in their minds, they also find themselves automatically adjusting to your own emotions as the speaker.

This is why you see yourself unconsciously frowning your face in support of the anger a speaker feels when narrating how he almost punched a pickpocket who tried to pick his last penny. You were not present during the event, but the kinds of adjectives, gestures, adverbs, facial expressions the speaker inputs into the narrative would overshadow you and you will only notice how angry you have been when he smiles and says "well, that's in the past..."

Your tone and mood, just as the behaviorist believe, elicit a certain response in the behaviors of the audience, that is, their corresponding responses. Your tone and mood during your presentation determine the response you would get in return.

Elements that dictate tone and mood during presentation

Dressing: Your dressing during a presentation could determine how serious your audience might take you. Formal presentations require you being formal in your dressing while looking as professional as possible. At the same time, presentations that require you to be in a light atmosphere demand that you be a little bit informal in your dressing while retaining the professional purpose of your presentation.

Introduction: From your introduction, your audience can calculate how sound you are with what you are about to discuss and they can make the decision in that instance whether to give their attention to you or not. Apart from this, the feel of an introduction determines how your presentation would look from the beginning to the end, except you swerve along the way. Hitting their curiosity from the start earns you their attention till you've cleared their doubts and passed your message across simultaneously.

Intonation: As discussed earlier, your intonation could suggest your intended meaning and perceivable meanings to your audience. Therefore, inappropriate intonation could affect an unwanted result, while the right intonation would bring about the desired result.

Language (diction): Your choice of words at times could determine the level of responsiveness your audience would give during presentation. Setting your language to fit the linguistic levels of your audience would be of advantage to you, hence the need to carry out enough research before commencing. And remember not to be too technical and correct, niche jargons can appear boring and make them lose interest in the topic.

Nonverbal inputs (facial expressions, gestures, distance between the speaker and the audience): These are also important determinants of how engaging your presentation could be. When you stir up certain emotions in your audience as a result of your facial expressions and body gestures they can relate with, you will discover that comprehension and retention becomes easier on their parts.

CONCLUSION

"No one became a loyal client because of an ad. They become loyal clients because of direct contact" –
Kenyetta L. Gordon

Building a fast and smart relationship with a potential customer begins with effective communication and the continuous relationship between you still involves effective communication. Effective communication should be implemented in every part of a buyer's journey from the awareness stage to the decision-making stage. You must, at one point or another, communicate value, preach your brand, communicate offers, and communicate assurance at intervals. The impact of communication in marketing cannot be overemphasized, and only the best communicators make the best out of this process.